The De

Settled

Peace

After Forgiveness

by

Henrietta Bowen

ISBN- 979-8-218-14986-4

Liberation's Publishing LLC
West Point - Mississippi

The Deep
Settled

Peace

After Forgiveness

Henrietta Bowen

Table of Content

Let me introduce myself ...

My name is Henrietta Bowen, and a COVID-19 survivor. It is my desire that you enjoy this comfortable read which is long overdue, how the Almighty God miraculously rescued me from the clutches of COVID-19 in the year 2021.

I had no recollection of what transpired while I was a patient in the hospital for 19 days, but the medical team suggested that I go directly from the hospital to a nursing home facility equipped to provide physical therapy to complete my treatment and recovery.

One thing I remembered when I left the nursing home facility was that I had a burning desire to inform everyone about the goodness of God and to further stressed that God is Real, based on all my experiences as you read: "The Deep Settled Peace... after forgiveness." My proof for you that God is real.

Let's go!

Before I Forgot 🌿

To say I am uniquely blessed is an understatement, because the life that I live as a child of God for over thirty-eight years speaks volumes. Praying for others is my passion, especially for the sick, because they cannot pray for themselves in critical moments. Reading my Bible throughout the day has escalated my spiritual ego immensely, especially when I learned that praying for others is also biblical. While sharing and giving to others and being a blessing to whoever I found in need, my life was interrupted by COVID-19. It struck in September of 2021 and plagued me through October of the same year. What I suffered in those short months is going to blow your mind, and I will tell of how THE ALMIGHTY GOD RESCUED ME MIRACULOUSLY!" I pray that after reading my testimony you will walk away knowing that God is a pleasant help in a time of trouble.

Just when the enemy thought he had me down; the almighty God rescued me from the jaws of COVID-19, and as a result of what I suffered I was empowered with an undeniable amazing testimony which revealed the true Deity of God. During this time, I also received a direct message from the Lord, "If everyone knew that God is Real, they would not be doing the things that they are doing." He listens to our conversations. He assists us when we are in trouble. He never leaves us alone after we accept Him as our Lord and Savior.

I remembering it being a cold morning in January when I placed the key into the ignition and started the car. I began to pray as I drove along the road for the safety of myself and everyone I would encounter, everyone who occupied the roads, the seas, the skies, the rails, the truck drivers, bus drivers, police giving chase, children crossing for school. I prayed for innocent people crossing the street. This was how I directed my prayers whenever I was driving. My list goes on and on. Once at work I pray for my co-workers and supervisors. There is so much work to be done by the people of God.

I developed this habit of praying while driving and going about my day because one morning while praying at home, I got carried away in prayer. After that I kept doing it daily. Prayer is what I do, even to this day. I have given up driving for myself, but I do enjoy praying for others and it becomes a habit. Whenever I see an ambulance or a fire truck with its emergency lights on, I always raise my hand to their direction and say a quick prayer on their behalf. Sincere prayers work and words are powerful. We have not, because we ask not. That has proven to be true.

I'm an encourager and very passionate about reading the Bible and praying for others which generates some positive results from time to time. I thrive on a good praise report and look forward to draw from my spiritual well, the Bible. I am a person of strong faith and belief in God; hence I became extremely passionate about reading the entire Bible from cover to cover. That was truly the desire of my heart. Now, back to my cold January morning event.

As I drove to a stop light, about four miles from home, I

suddenly felt dizzy, and my heart was beating fast. It was very convenient for me to pull off the road, so I took the opportunity to do so. Things happened fast, it was a good thing my husband was home. I called him first and told him what happened and asked him to hurry and come get me. I was feeling worse and worse. My next phone call was to my office. I spoke to my supervisor and told her how I felt. My husband was on his way to get me. I planned to go to the doctor as soon as his office was opened. It was early in the morning, so they had enough time to cover my shift. I went to my family doctor later in the morning and he sent me to the hospital to get some x-rays and other tests. I'm diabetic and have high blood pressure so it was a bit complicated. This also kept me from being diagnosed correctly starting off.

Later, I went to my office and permanently resigned my post, just to be on the safe side. I was already semi-retired and working only two days per week. I had no problem with retiring, but I didn't like being alone at home with my daughter and husband going off to work every day. It left me with a not so good feeling. How did I solve this dilemma? I volunteered at my neighborhood hospital. I started feeling unwell at work. My husband had to come and get me a few times. I ended up having to take indefinite time off from volunteering also. This was a year before the COVID-19 Delta Variant arrived.

While at home the first few months were lonely. My excitement for cooking brought my joy back. I created some special recipes, because I was always an excellent cook and baker. I also enjoyed switching around the kitchen décor. Our kitchen smelt like a millionaire's gourmet kitchen! Our house was immaculately clean, until I got very tired sometimes from taking on a little too much. During my down time, I read the Bible. I preferred to read with a reading partner so that we could compare notes. Iron does sharpen Iron.

Another undertaking I took on was removing the bad weeds from our garden and nourishing it with fresh soil and water. This was done mostly in the evenings and on the weekends. My husband and I enjoyed doing things together, I wished he was retired as well. Watching seeds planted into the soil and waiting for them to grow was a new form of excitement. It was mind blowing to watch them grow to maturity. We enjoyed many organic vegetables from our backyard garden. Our rose garden in the front of our home was beautiful, and still is. Joggers would slow down to get a better view of the clustered bunches of pink roses. We received many compliments from our rose garden.

This became my norm until after several months COVID-19 gained strength and showed up just about everywhere until it reached the company my husband worked with. It is a hug company that operates worldwide. One of the staff members even died from COVID-19 in another state. The HR department in my husband's state took precautions by sending home the older staff with high-risk problems such as diabetes and high blood pressure. He was sixty-three years old and matched the description. He was approached and agreed to their request to stay home for three months. That was the month of March 2020.

He was relieved to come home, no one wanted to be around COVID-19. He received another quote to take a year off if he chose to. That quote was followed by an email from HR with a package deal for two years pay with health insurance paid up unto his retirement age of sixty-five. That offer was too good to refuse. He accepted it and it went into effect August 1, 2020. Are you thinking what I'm thinking? On the previous page I mentioned that I would like my husband to retire. We are now learning that when we put our trust in God, he will grant us our heart's desire. I was tickled pink when I discovered that my husband was retired and to say that I was ecstatic was a truly understated. Happiness took over my retirement plans completely as I disclosed my desires to my husband and reading partner because it happened exactly as I wished, my God is real.

My husband was thrilled to be home with me as well, because I was always complaining about how lonely I was at home by myself. Of course, there was no guilt on him for an early retirement, because it was not his idea. He only complied with HR emails and management. He received a very large envelope with his retirement information, package deal and several other documents. His official retirement plaque arrived in the mail later in the year. There were now two retirees from a family of three leaving only one worker that does not drive. Our daughter does not drive so her parents are delighted to take her to and from work. Since we are on a permanent vacation, she gets to make our vacation decisions.

We wore our masks and never left home without them from the time COVID-19 began. During the month of August 2021, our daughter who lives in Antigua was visiting with us for the first time and we were busy shopping with her as well as showing her around. One evening when we picked up our daughter from work, she said that she was not feeling well because she had to work for someone else who was off, and that person works in the freezer. So, I told her to let them know that she has never worked in the freezer before, and it makes you sick. The following evening when we went to get her from work, for some unknown reason, we all forgot our masks. Neither of us were wearing a mask. Can you believe it? That was the first time since COVID-19 that my husband and I ever left the house without our masks. Wait a minute it gets worse.

As soon as she entered the vehicle, she let loose a powerful sneeze that caused everyone, except dad, to dive while searching for a mask that we always carried in the vehicle. She also let us know that she heard someone at her job had come down with COVID-19. That was news no one wanted to hear. The next day she tested positive for COVID-19. Of course, me and my bold self, volunteered to take care of her while she quarantined. You know, the perfect one that always wears her mask and gloves. Dad took care of our visiting adult daughter. They both got tested and had COVID-19 as well.

Yours truly refused to get tested. I had no symptoms at all. The next morning I passed by her room and the door was opened. I rushed in her room and changed her bed linens, not realizing that I was not wearing a mask or gloves. Wow, did I get my share. When I got finished, I felt weary and stuffy. I always wore my mask and gloves when I entered her room. As I went to remove my mask, I noticed that I was not wearing one neither any gloves. I always changed my clothes and took a shower after changing her linens, and I changed them every day. This day I didn't have enough energy to wash my hands. I could only crawl into the bed. From that moment on, I knew nothing about what was going on with my life until I was in the nursing home facility. I would have spent nineteen days in the hospital before this. The diabetes and high blood pressure magnified the symptoms of COVID-19. COVID got me good! But God!

My family and I decided not to take the vaccines which was a bad idea. The rest I am about to tell you is only hearsay, because I have no recollection of what took place after that morning. I was told that I would not eat much. I would ask for water and only took a sip before saying I had had enough. My husband called our family doctor, and he advised him to take me to the hospital emergency room and he would meet us there. My husband said that I even spoke with our doctor, but I don't recall it. They gave me a bath and got me all dressed up to go to the hospital but when I reached the top of the staircase I sat and refused to go downstairs. My daughter called 911. My husband said the ambulance arrived in less than ten minutes. Families were not allowed to go to the hospital during COVID-19, communications were done by phone.

One of my daughters from another mother, was a registered

nurse and lived in California, contacted the hospital where I was admitted in Georgia. She made inquiries and connected with my doctor and nurse because she was knowledgeable with my case. The link was productive, and my family was briefed on my conditions daily.

Recovery

My COVID-19 journey began on Thursday September 23, 2021. My symptoms with COVID worsen and my family had to call an ambulance to transport me to the hospital. Once there I was admitted. What I thought would take a few days turned into weeks and on Thursday, September 30, 2021, my family was contacted by the hospital's medical team to discuss my progress. They met in the chapel with one of my doctors and a nurse. The prognosis was not good. I had become unresponsive and was having other complications. The team suggested to my family that if there was no improvement, they should be prepared to do one of the following three choices:

1). Hospice

2). Nursing home care that offers 5 days per week therapy

3). Home care services where the insurance would only pay for 3 days of therapy per week.

That being said, my family went home and continued to pray for a miraculous recovery as they believed and trusted in God for my deliverance. Truly, I can honestly say that "God is Real," and He surely answers sincere prayers. I began to improve and started responding satisfactorily.

I was going to be released. I was improving. The hospital was getting ready to discharge me and requested that I should go to a nursing home facility equipped to provide physical therapy five days a week to complete my therapy and finish my recovery. My family selected option two from the three choices listed above. The nursing home facility would provide physical therapy, speech therapy and occupational therapy. So, after nineteen days in the hospital I was transferred to the nursing home on that Tuesday, October 12th. The transfer to the nursing home facility was a different atmosphere with no comparison to the hospital. There was no visiting accommodation at the hospital for a family member or a friend due to me being a COVID-19 patient.

God had another blessing. At the nursing home I received my own private room. My niece happened to be an administrator there. At first, I thought it was a coincidence, then again, we should not refer to the blessings of God as such. God is a provider for those who diligently seek Him. God provided me with my own private room, and my family and friends could visit with me. In fact, my husband and daughter visited with me during the eighteen days that I spent at the nursing home facility. My husband made me homemade soups and special smoothies which were always so delicious. One could not put a price on my family's visit, because it was PRICELESS!

Honestly, it was not possible to describe the joy that flooded my heart when I saw my husband and daughter walk into my room every evening. My husband smiled from ear to ear and his countenance always illuminated the room. I looked forward to his hugs and affection, but never looked forward to the goodbye when it was time to leave. Please understand that it was not easy for either party, but we had no choice when visiting time was over.

My daughter's gentle affectionate touch and the sparks in her eyes revealed that she felt more comfortable knowing that I would be coming home soon. She never missed a moment checking to see if I was comfortable, especially using the bathroom by myself. She showed me all the steps to follow to gain my confidence, instead of asking someone for assistance. She was phenomenally successful with her efforts. They stayed with me every night until visiting time was over.

My daughter's employer suggested that she should take all the time she needed to be with her parents until they could manage by themselves. She thought it over and decided that three months would be fine to be with her parents, so she thanked them and confirmed the date of her return. Her attention towards us was superb and exceeded all expectations. She is our special gift from God! My family and I were particularly impressed with the services rendered by the nursing home facility staff. The energetic atmosphere of the entire staff had nurtured and energized my speedy recovery along with sincere prayers from family and friends. There were divine interventions from God that I cannot explain, even if I try.

The three therapist departments in their respective places were terrific and all the other workers at the facility were very hospitable and kind to all my guests. My family and I extended our sincere gratitude to everyone who contributed to my successful recovery. My sincere thanks to our Niece Pastor Marcia Hines the

Administrator, for her morning visits whenever she was on duty: "Ms. Bowen, you are a miracle, and you are going to walk out of here." I cherished those words and looked forward to a positive result. She gave me hope which was much needed. Those encouraging words lingered on and I believed every word; then it happened exactly as she said. Thanks again for those encouraging words, and for saying goodbye every evening before you leave. Your positivity was an antidote to my recovery, and I thank you very much. God bless you!

This Impressive Team of Therapists Were Terrific

1. The physical therapist did a remarkable job who tolerated my complaints of being tired, and "do I have to do this now?" He assisted me with the walker for just a little before I managed independently. I walked faster than he had anticipated and was overly impressed with my success. It was a challenge to climb the stairs of fifteen steps on day seventeen, prior to my discharge on the 18th when all my therapists were satisfied with my accomplishments.

2. The speech therapist was quite knowledgeable and kind. She gained my confidence in a remarkable way. By the end of my grading period: Her last day with me, she said, "if you were in my class at school, I would have given you an A+" which was an amazing compliment that brings back memories because I was an A+ student at school in my classes.

3. The occupational therapist came in incredibly early in the morning just when the sleep was extremely good. Woke me up and assisted me in washing myself and getting all dressed up, then I would go back to bed and slept until breakfast. She executed her job in a unique and professional way. I always looked forward to seeing her smiling face in the mornings. Beautiful smiles, especially in the medical field are more than rubies and diamonds and are strong antidotes for early recovery.

The caseworker and therapists assessed my progress because I was miraculously improving daily. Yes, I said "miraculously" because it was true. My three therapists: physical therapist, speech therapist and occupational therapist, were utterly amazed at my remarkable progress. They agreed that they had never seen anyone recovered this fast from my condition when I arrived at the facility.

I was completely DEPENDENT with ADL'S, gait and required assistance with everything! My diet was puree and nectar liquids while I was in the facility. I went from being non-ambulatory to being able to climb the stairs of fifteen steps in 17 days. One of the staff said, "Not in my six years of working here, I had never seen anyone recover this fast and was heading home." She mentioned how cheerful I was and added, "everyone around here are going to miss you."

Another staff member who entered my room said, "it was truly an honor to have someone like you in our facility." I had politely thanked everyone for all the kind hospitality that they had shown to me and my family before they exited my room. One thing, I never forget to tell everyone how good God has been to me. I have had staff members walk up to me and said "Mrs. Bowen, we are surely going to miss you."

My insurance provider and the social worker went ahead and made the necessary arrangements with a reputable home healthcare agency that provided the appropriate home care services, which would be necessary. They scheduled an oxygen tank with a small portable, along with a walker that I should receive at my home to assist with my complete recovery.

The oxygen tank and portable unit arrived on time, but the walker arrived one week later because it was on a back order. Good thing that I was recovering miraculously because I was walking around the house safely downstairs. I went from the nursing home facility early on Friday morning, October 29, 2021, escorted to our SUV in a wheelchair driven by one of their amazing professional nurses and my husband assisted me into the vehicle. When I arrived home, I headed directly to my recliner which I was so happy to see.

Upon arrival home, I received a call from the home healthcare services and we scheduled a home visit appointment for Monday morning, November 1, 2021. The assessor was a female registered nurse. She arrived on time and politely explained the company's policies and what I needed to do. It was a remarkably successful meeting that lasted about an hour.

I later found out that a physical therapist will be my coach one day per week through Thursday, December 16, 2021. He also arrived a week late because he did not get the work order from his office. Is this a trend that the walker and the physical therapist were both one week late? Hold that thought! God had a miraculous plan for that delayed week.

A visiting nurse came once per week to record my progress which was the norm. I had already done my own shower, pedicure and manicure the day before the assessor arrived, and was also in my kitchen cooking up a storm the day before our meeting. Getting back to my stove was a major antidote because I enjoyed cooking and baking. I tried to be careful by checking out all my surroundings. No climbing on the stool nor stooping in the kitchen to retrieve any items from the pantry.

My assessor told me that based on my progress I only need physical therapy for my feet. During that period, I had to be incredibly careful when I walked around the house because the walker would be arriving one week late. It was obvious that I would no longer need a walker because I was doing quite well without it. No other service was required because I was recovering faster than the norm.

Henrietta Bowen

Photo Request for Newsletter 🌿

Upon learning of my fast improvement, how I was climbing my staircase at home a few days after I was discharged from the nursing home facility, the nursing home administrative requested permission in writing for me to send a photo of me taken at the top of my staircase because they would like to feature my fast progress report into one of their monthly newsletters. The hospitality at the facility was superb, so there was no hesitancy to fulfill their request; So the requirement was honored immediately.

TRUE STORY!!!

Over five years ago, I purchased a size ten dress that I loved so much but at the time of purchase I was a size fourteen. Funny enough, my husband liked the dress as well, and he agreed and said he know that I would make it happen. As soon as the photo request came my husband said:

"Honey, do you think you should try and see if you could fit into that special dress that you had been holding for years? I responded, "Yes, let me try it on!!" The dress was perfect because I had lost so much weight and it was perfect for the photoshoot. It was a classic!!

The partial newspaper!

This patient was the aunt of our nursing home administrator. She was a patient in the hospital with COVID and was completely DEPENDENT with ADL'S, gait belt among other issues, and required assistance with everything! Her diet was change to puree and nectar liquids while she was in the facility. The patient went from being non-ambulatory to being able to climb the stairs of fifteen steps in seventeen days before she went home on day eighteen. Of course, there were more to the story they wrote, but I got this information from a folded copy of the newsletter that I received in a text. I was hoping to get my own copy but that never happened. However, I was grateful for this information because I had no prior records, nor recollection of my condition when I arrived at the Facility.

CELEBRATE *With Me*

Genesis
Rehab Services
Improving lives every day.

November 2021
Delmar Gardens of Gwinnett- Lawrenceville, GA

To reach our goals, we often have to take a lot of steps to get there. This was certainly the case for Henrietta Bowen. After a hospitalization related to COVID-19, she found herself unable to walk and dependent on others to help her complete basic daily tasks, such as dressing and bathing. She even found it difficult to eat, resulting in the need for a puree diet with thickened liquids for safety. With hard work and dedication Henrietta re-wrote her story. At discharge she was walking again and even able to climb 15 steps! She returned to her normal diet and her normal life. Great job Henrietta!

Henrietta Bowen

The Miraculous

Nobody thought I would be able to go upstairs like I normally did, anytime soon, although I had already gone upstairs a couple of times before; but God had a major miraculous plan for me, that would undoubtedly blow my mind. On Thursday November 11, I had a 9:00 am appointment with my physical therapist and decided to go upstairs to take a shower before my appointment. We started out from downstairs at 8:06 am heading towards upstairs; with my husband following behind me, I held onto the rail with my right hand and lifted my left foot and placed it on the first step, then I did the same with my right foot which I also placed on the first step. Bravo, I just climbed the first step, and heading towards the top of the stairs.

After repeating this method for the third time I was on step number three, and got a little weary along the way, I asked my husband how long he think I would have this discomfort in climbing the stairs and he said, "God will take care of it, babe." I climbed another two steps and I felt worse, so I stepped backwards and leaned back on the rail and made another two steps using the same method, at this point I felt very weary, and could not go up nor down; So I said, "Herb, what should I do? Should I go down or up?" and he said "UP!"

I paused, tried to snap out of the weariness and made a giant step towards upstairs, then I suddenly started to WALK NORMALLY. Herb was not only shocked, but he had to process what he had just witnessed as he hastened to catch up with me to get to the shower. My brain kicked into high gear as it raced towards my appointment time. I took my shower standing as usual, although it was different with me having to use the handheld showerhead, but the change was great! Prior to this amazing miracle that had just happened, Herb and my daughter had already rearranged the bathroom by installing a bath stool which arrived the evening before. He also replaced the stationary shower head with a handheld shower to accommodate a more comfortable shower. Little did they know that God had a better idea while they were making all those plans.

Shower and hygiene went speedily, I did my own lotion and deodorant, fixed my hair, and rushed downstairs like I did normally. I was on time and the physical therapist was on time. Earlier on, you might have remembered that my ordered walker, and assigned physical therapist were both late for a week. Now, it had become obvious that God does not need any help to execute His formidable powers. God is Real and does not share His Glory with anyone. Hence, a walker was no longer necessary because our God does amazing things.

God did miraculous things in my life which was hard to explain because nobody would believe me. If I need a certain item, I would, get it before I ask the Lord for it. Sometimes I would just laugh and say, "Father God, you are all together wonderful." Then, I remembered that God knows the desires of our hearts. There was another scheduled appointment by a registered nurse for 12:00 noon on this same day. Her salutation was brilliant but among other attributes, she mentioned that she thought she was coming to see a little old lady, but she was amazed with my poise and appearance. Her compliments reigned supreme. My overall appearance was quite shocking. I later told her of my miracle that took place earlier in the morning.

My nurse observed and realized that I had documented my vital signs and logged them to date and noticed that I had kept a permanent record of all my meds, and everything was in perfect order. She said, "you do not require our services because you are on top of things." She recommended that I only needed the assistance of a physical therapist and that she would inform her office of the vast improvement that I had made, contrary to their records.

While she was talking with me, my phone rang and there was an occupational therapist calling to make an appointment to come and give me a shower. We were on the speaker phone and after I promptly told her that I was doing my own shower. I did my own pedicure and manicure the second day after I arrived home. That was the second time she called. The nurse said that if she comes you could probable give her a shower instead; jokingly of course.

I had miraculously recovered from my sickness, and I cannot explain it to anyone, but one thing I do know is that I will not, and cannot leave God out of the picture, because only He can work in this manner. No medicine can take credit for my recovery because I am at a loss for words. I had dedicated my life to the True and Living God and He is sustaining me with His Grace and Mercy because I put my faith and trust in Him.

Also, taking into consideration, the amount, of prayers that went up for my speedy recovery. Talk about speed, it was a lightning recovery! Again, my sincere gratitude for all the telephone calls and prayers. Contrary to the report that sent to the home healthcare agency about my condition; there is no doubt in my mind that my total recovery was nothing short of miracles from God. So, when I tell you that my recovery was miraculous, you should believe me! These miracles are indelible in my heart!

Faith in God with Sincere Prayer Works!!

I would like to inform all my readers that SINCERE prayer works, and I would encourage them to try it. We should pray for each other because when they are sick, they cannot pray. A sick person cannot think straight, and sometimes cannot think at all. We had to depend on others to pray for us. Sincere prayer is not about just calling words, it is more than that. Faith and Trust in God works together.

We must put our trust in God one hundred percent, ninety-nine and a half is not good enough. He will not settle for seconds. I told my husband that I love him very much, and he knows that too, because action speaks louder than words. I begged him, not to love me more than he loves the Lord God Almighty, and on that note, we agreed that it was the right thing to do and would have it no other way.

Ever since we made that decision, our lives had never been the same. We had re-dedicated our lives to Jesus Christ through faith and prayers and desired to search the Scriptures for Biblical knowledge about our blueprint which is the Holy Bible. Before going further, let me give you a brief synopsis on why I authored this book to encourage others that God is Real, and He hears and answers prayers.

This pandemic brought my husband and I much closer to God. I was retired before my husband and to say that I was lonely at home when my husband and daughter left for work in the mornings was truly an understatement. Although I was struggling with type 2 diabetes and high blood pressure, I was volunteering at the hospital, one day per week, on my husband's day off. It was difficult for me and was not feeling well on the job. Twice my husband had to take me home. So I took an indefinite time off.

I got in the habit of reading my Bible while I was at home and pray especially for the sick. During that time, I felt eager to read the entire Bible because I always had a feeling that there was something special that I needed to know about the Bible for myself. I made previous attempts but failed; and always felt that something was not connecting. I read the Scriptures during the day, but not starting from Genesis. I needed a reading partner. However, I always had that burning desire to achieve that goal.

On or about the end of March during COVID-19, my husband's employer decided that his medical condition was a considerable risk for him and suggested that he could take time off from work, up to a year. So he gladly accepted the offer. By this time the country was on lock down and his HR department sent him an e-mail which he could not resist, instructing him that because of his high-risk condition and the severity of COVID-19, they would encourage him to take an early retirement with a package deal, an offer too good to refuse.

He accepted it with extraordinary joy! That was the miraculous e-mail I was waiting on! God to my rescue! I was lonely at home and needed a Bible reading partner too. Thank you Lord! My God is an on-time GOD! He may not come when you want Him, but He is always on time. Had my husband made that early retirement request at the time when I asked him to; he would not have gotten the package deal for two years of medical insurance. So you see, when you pray for God's favor, and He delayed your request; just keep the faith and continue to put your trust in Him. There is no doubt in my mind that God answers prayers.

God is always working out something better in your favor. The effective date for his early retirement was August 1, 2020. That was another prayer which God had answered for me. I was so ecstatic with that decision because I always yearned for my husband to be retired. God is hugely impressive. He may not come when we want him, but He is always on time. Let your request known unto God, and He will give you the desires of your heart. After seeing all my prayers answered, don't you think He will do the same thing for you as well?

Reading the Bible throughout its entirety was always our

passion but attempts made and failed because we took the wrong approach. Finally, we spoke to the Lord about our concerns, and He made things happened for us. As you read on a little further, you will discover how God is waiting to give us the desires of our hearts only for the asking. I will always repeat and declare that God is truly real!

Having my husband home with me, Praise God; was an amazing answer to my prayers! Now that I have a permanent reading partner, it makes all the difference. We also knew that reading from Geneses through Revelation was not the right way to go. We spoke to the Lord about our concerns, and we discussed it openly and the Lord did a remarkable job by revealing the answer that we needed in a unique way. Here is the scoop!

The date when all this happened has slipped my mind, but when I glanced on the clock, it was exactly 5:00 am when I woke up, which seemed rather unusual because I normally woke up at 6:00 am to do my vital signs, but after glancing at the clock, I sat up with my feet dangling towards the floor and quietly got up and went to the bathroom although I had no urge to use it.

As I sat on the toilet while the lid was still down, as if I was waiting for some marching orders, still had no idea why I was sitting there; I stared at the Bible in front of me that is kept on top of the launder basket, which I enjoyed reading every day, instead of reading a magazine. I leaned over and picked it up and opened it. To my surprise, it did not open where the Scriptures were; instead, it opened at the back. Upon discovering this information, I had to wipe my eyes to see what was staring back at me.

My readers, I kid you not!!! When I saw:

"52-Week Bible Reading Plan"

I was ecstatic to learn that the information we needed was into the back of our Bible all this time. Nicely arranged, exactly how I would like to read the Holy Bible with the Old and New Testaments mixed for a better understanding of the Scriptures. Would you agree with me by saying, God is amazing! God listens to our conversations, so let us govern ourselves accordingly. God is Real. I have had reasons to be convinced.

Memories on Recorded Supernatural Miracles

Please allow me to jog your memory a little bit. Do you recall when I was climbing the staircase earlier on and felt weary along the way, when I asked my husband how long he thinks I would have this discomfort in climbing the stairs, and his response was, "God will take care of it, babe." Now, would you agree with me when I said that God listens to our conversations? If my calculation was right, I was about thirty seconds away from an eyewitness miracle of a lifetime!

God allowed me to walk normally, so fast that my husband had to hurry to keep up with me. I have heard testimonies of miracles, and I had also read about miracles, but I had never experienced one live and direct, with my husband by my side as an eyewitness. It was a supernatural experience which I will never forget. There were so many miraculous things that were happening to me that I was unable to explain to anyone.

I found myself walking normally around the house immediately after I went home from the facility. I was using a walker at the facility and could remember holding on to my husband's arm on that morning. However, the Good Lord allowed me to walk in my house without a walker, and without holding on to any object whatsoever. My God is utterly amazing!

All Things Are Possible with God

On the second day of my arrival home, I washed my hair and did my own pedicure and manicure that were in extremely bad shape. Think of me spending nineteen days in a hospital and an additional eighteen days in a nursing home facility, not mentioning the fact that I kept putting it off prior to these events because of the pandemic.

It was extra work for me, but I felt so proud that I called myself; "the brand new me!" Only God could have made that possible. To this day, I wondered how did I do it? Then I remembered that we should let our requests known unto God and He will grant us the desires of our hearts. We need to read, understand, believe, and apply the written words of God, because they are for our edification. Upon the completion of our Biblical assignments, each of us should all conclude that God is Real.

Please do not forget that God listens to our conversations, and I am strongly recommending that we keep our conversations clean because there is an all- seeing eye that is watching over us, and ears that hears. You must believe me when I tell you that God is Real and would like to communicate with us only at our invitation. Read our Bible and pray for others always. We should confess our faults to the Lord, and ask His forgiveness daily, bearing in mind that all have sinned and become short of the glory of God.

Reading The Bible Throughout Its Entirety

Our official Bible reading began on the same day of our amazing discovery of: "How to read through the Bible in 52 weeks." The reading plan was already set in place for us, so we just followed the guidelines. We were extremely fascinated because the Old and New Testament were exactly as we had desired. We read threw challenging chapters in the first setting but planned to go easy for the long haul; except for short stories.

Reading as a team was a marvelous idea. Pausing for breaks were always exceptional, because that was our discussion time when we reviewed and compared notes, and highlights. Our most challenging Scriptures were in the Old Testament, which we planned to re-visit, but sometimes we got the answers from other chapters. It was indeed a pleasure reading the Bible with a planned schedule.

The poetry, history, proverb, prophecy, songs, letters, and apocalyptic literature of the Bible provides the reader with wonder and enjoyment. We discovered that reading the Bible was exciting, captivating, inspiring and humorous! But when we allowed the Holy Spirit to speak to us through God's Words, our reading crosses from mere enjoyment to life transformation. After reading the Bible throughout its entirety we can honestly say our lives have changed.

Henrietta Bowen

The Clutches of COVID Began 🌿

Our daughter who lives in Antigua was visiting with us for the first time, and we went shopping and showing her around. Fortunately, it was not a distraction from our reading schedules. After supper was our reading time! Nothing could separate us from our Bibles. At least, that was what we thought, until I felt so sick that my family had to call the ambulance on September 23, that took me to the hospital. I had already told my COVID-19 survival story, but this was when it all started, so this little synopsis will serve as a constant reminder of how real God was and still is, to me every day.

There goes our reading partnership for another few months, after God had miraculously saved my life from the clutches of COVID-19 Delta Variant. You will discover that God is Real, after you get through reading about my journey and testimony as a COVID-19 Survivor story. During your reading you might be wondering why the writer kept repeating that: "Our God is truly Real," because He really is! My entire sickness and recovery depicted miraculous events daily.

My husband and I are retired and are inseparable, but unfortunately, I spent nineteen days in the hospital, and there was no visitation allowed for any family or friends of COVID-19 patients; but thank goodness, the hospital suggested that I should be transferred to a reputable Nursing Home facility that was equipped with physical therapy, speech therapy and occupational therapy for

5 days per week which was required to complete my recovery.

Discharged from Hospital into Nursing Home

All arrangements confirmed and transferred directly to the nursing home facility on Tuesday October 12, 2021. It was indeed a very reputable nursing home facility, much more than I had anticipated. The therapists did exceptionally well in their respective places, and so were all the nurses, and staff members. The technicians who maintain the facility were unique and extremely hospitable to my family and friends.

I got my own private room which allowed my family and friends to visit with me. It was a pleasure to see my daughter Yvonne, son Keno and his wife Ruth, and our dear friend Gayle who came to visit with me. There were absolutely no words to express the joy that I felt, when my husband and my daughter who is living at home with us, arrived. The smiles on their faces and the warmth of their touch, were indeed the precise antidote for my complete recovery. Travel distance from home to the nursing home facility was approximately fifty-six miles, round trip; I spent 18 days at the facility, and they came every day!

During my health crisis my daughter's job encouraged her to take all the time she needed to assist her parents, so she took 3 months off from work. Having our adult daughter at home with us for three months was an amazing experience. She was a tower of strength, and we savored every moment. we enjoyed shopping and had fun times together. Preparing her favorite dishes and soups were fun to watch especially when we got to taste them, because we are diabetics and tried to stay within our salt and sugar limits. Dad and I enjoyed cooking, so we really spent superior quality, family times together, that we never had before, because of the usual work schedules.

Reading the Scriptures Brings Out the Impressive Wonder of God

Reading the Scriptures were our goal, so we continued and discovered that, reading the Bible brings out the impressive wonder of God as He spoke to, and loved the humanity He created. Because Christ is the incarnation of God, the New Testament should be prominent in any Bible reading plan. This encouraged our appetite for the undiluted words of God.

As we studied the complexity of the nature of God as recorded in both the Old and New Testaments, we developed a clearer understanding of what He desired in our relationships to others and to Him. He desired for us to be in touch with others and to treat each other with love and respect, pray for each other. There are people who condoles "me, myself, and I." God disallowed that!

He laid it out noticeably clear that we MUST include "OTHERS" in our prayers and in everything we do. That is another reason it is important to read the Bible throughout its entirety, because sometimes we tend to forget the tiny details. I had never noticed the intensity of "OTHERS," but God makes it plain, because, every time He gets a chance, He mentioned it.

It also revealed the impressive provisions that God had reserved for humanity. Knowing that this information is available to every reader of this book. I am strongly recommending that everyone should grasp this opportunity before it is too late. It is imperative that everyone should read the Bible primarily to avoid the mistakes that we regretted. Thanks for Salvation and forgiveness, through Grace and Mercy. The Blood that Jesus Christ sheds on that Cruel Cross of Calvary, made it all possible.

The Bible that we read, holds the answer to humanity's past, present and future. It is a wellspring of wisdom and divine instruction, and this well never runs dry. We should draw from this spring daily, to find direction and purpose for our lives. Reading the Bible will convict and encourage you to pray and ask God's forgiveness if you had never prayed before. It is a soul-searching experience that allows us to identify all our shortcomings. I would be rather selfish, if I hoarded this wealth of information to myself, which was for all humanity.

After we were fully engaged in reading the Bible and confirmed that God wants to be first in our lives and will not settle for second place. He said that He is a Jealous God and will not share His Glory with another. People love their cars, houses, jobs, bank accounts, jewels, properties, fame, education, wives, husbands, children, and others. We cannot put all these things before God because He will have none of that! Everything we own belongs to God. We obtained all this information by reading the Scriptures. I would like everyone to read the Holy Bible throughout its entirety, for their own edification. Truth is, we were astonished when we finished reading the Bible.

Now that we have discovered the absolute truth that we yearned for over the years, it has become evident that changes in our lives immediately was necessary. So, we invited God to come into our home, into the vehicle we drive and everywhere we go. Divine protection was an absolute requirement, and we never waited for a special occasion to pray, because it was our daily commitment. Our prayer lives had increased, especially for the sick and praying for others became a priority, and prayer requests had increased tremendously. Yes, we made changes which were necessary because one cannot read the Scriptures and remain the same.

Everyone should establish a relationship with God where we could tell Him all our problems, with the assurance that He would not share it with a best friend. When we give God First place in our lives, He will take us places that we have never dreamed. He does not share His Glory with anyone and will not settle for second place. You will find this information when you read the Bible.

We should all ask God to forgive others who wronged us. Likewise, we should not forget to ask God to forgive our sins before attempting to pray for others, because He will not answer our prayers if we have un-forgiveness in our heart. Sincere prayers really work. Strong faith, and trust in God is a necessity for our Spiritual growth.

Our daily reading is of vital importance because we gained spiritual strength as we study the Scriptures. Without faith, it is impossible to please God. There is no doubt in my mind that our faith in God is growing stronger each day. The story of Shadrach, Meshach and Abednego, whose faith in the book of (Daniel Chapter 3 KJV) was a classic example of faith in action. We read about others with strong faith, but The Fiery Furnace story had surely kicked our faith into high gear!

Forgiveness Is a Classic Antidote 🌿

In my walk with God, I tried to encourage everyone in my circle and whomever I get the chance to communicate with, about the importance of forgiveness. We must forgive others because we can benefit from it. One could not be stressed if there was nothing to be stressed about, because forgiveness takes care of that. Hence, better health and less sickness. When the heart is clean there will be no room for corruption in it.

We all know that cancers and other internal diseases caused through stress, and unwillingness to forgive. This is so sad; everyone should examine themselves. Be happy for others who have, and pray for their success, and while you are at it, take time out and thank God for what you have; by doing so, God will bless you with more.

Unforgiveness is a curable disease called stubborn which is curable by a simple antidote called prayer. Remember that only God can forgive Sin. All we need to do is pray a sincere prayer to God, asking Him to forgive the person who did us wrong, likewise, make the same request for ourselves. Be sincere from our heart when we pray because God already knows our thoughts.

It takes more muscles to frown than to smile, so let us be happy and keep smiling. It is of vital importance that we stop worrying about the things we do not have and instead, give thanks to God for what we already have. Keep on praising God by sending the praises up, and the blessings of God will come down. God already knows what we need and will grant us the desires of our hearts. Keep your focus on praying for others and your blessings will come to you in abundance, that you will always have enough to give.

Be kind to everyone because it is much better to give than to receive. Get in the habit of giving not only to your friends, but to others. Keep in mind that everybody needs something or someone. A beautiful smile, a kind compliment, or could be opening or holding the door for someone, but whatever you do in life, remember that it is more profitable to give, than to receive.

You would be surprised to know what would make somebody happy. Our God is an impressive provider, who always keep His promises and He never changes. We should all find time to read the Holy Bible and discover the plans that God has for humanity. If you give God a chance in your life, you will prove it for yourself that He is real, and what He did for me and my family, He will certainly do the same for you and yours.

You might have already learnt that I love to cook, and bake. Often, I would prepare a nice meal and invite someone or a family to come over to have dinner with my family. I also like to bake cakes and cookies and nice cheesecakes and other desserts. Even cutting my son's schoolmates hair was a gift because they always liked the way I cut his hair, and I was delighted to render my services to them when they came home with us after church.

I remembered one Sunday at Christmas time that I baked my special cakes and sliced them and had them wrapped individually and I gave them to one of my sons, on our way to Church, and asked him to give each package to the other kids that were not his friends, who came home with him sometimes. I was teaching him the importance of giving, not only to his friends.

The Bible instructed us that we should pray for others. Friendship and kindness are two different entities. A friend is always receiving from his friend, but when you give to someone that is not your friend it is more profitable, and one should give without expecting anything in return. The joy of giving will bless your soul.

The Blessings of God Through Extended Families

My husband and I are grateful for the love we shared with others we have met during our walk with God, through our Lord and Savior Jesus Christ with precious sons and daughters, nieces and nephews who addresses us as mom, dad, auntie, and uncle. This all happened because we try to do it God's way, by extending the true Agape love mixed with kindness. A kind word and a captivating smile from the heart, can last a lifetime. Our sincere gratitude to all our extended families near and far.

Our daughter Claudia who is a registered nurse and lives and works in California was also deeply knowledgeable with COVID-19 cases. She contacted the hospital that I was a patient in, and because of her experience in that area, was able to contact my doctors and nurses. During her daily communications with them, she expressed her concerns about my care, and was able to review my progress. She was a tower of strength to the family and was able to communicate my progress report daily to Dad and the rest of our family. This was an amazing blessing from one of our extended families! To God be the glory!

So, there you see a daughter from another mother who was able to comfort her extended family. She took time out of her busy schedule in California to contact my doctors and nurses at the Hospital in Atlanta where I was a patient. She also offered instructions for my total care as well because she was knowledgeable with my situation. The doctors and nurses, and her dad and family thanked her. That is true love in action, through loving kindness from someone who always give, especially praying for others, and not expecting anything in return. That is the Agape Love I am talking about. That is how God wants us to live for others.

By extending unconditional love through reading the Scriptures we obtained mercy from a nurse who took care of our medical concerns in crucial times. God makes provision for us in every area of our lives when we apply His principles. There are Biblical principles and guidelines for us to follow, that is why we are encouraging all our readers to search the Scriptures for themselves. You will be amazed of your discovery. Give it a chance, you have nothing to lose and everything to gain. We are so grateful that we did!!

God had blessed my husband and I with enough resources that we could afford to share with others, who sometimes wondered why we are so kind. We were always excited to share the blessings of God with others. There were no strings attached to our sharing. We were just kind people who believes in doing things God's way. Of course, we are now retired and not that energetic, but that does not change our love for giving.

Our passion for sharing with others comes from the heart not from feelings. The blessings of God will make room to receive more blessings to share. God inhabits the praises of His people, so when we send the praises up, more blessings will come down. We also promote the importance of reading our Bibles throughout its entirety, because it is our manual/blueprint which holds the answer to humanity's past, present, and future, with wisdom and divine instruction. Read it daily and find directions and purpose for your life.

It is a wealth of knowledge that everyone should experience. You will learn of your requirements from the Lord, and the plans He has for you. You cannot read the Bible throughout its entirety and remain the same! There are no limits to the blessings of God. We could tap into the resources provided for us, the undiluted words of God for ourselves, to discover the formidable plan that our Father God had prepared for us.

During my youthful days in Sunday School classes, I learnt the story about the three Hebrew Boys, but not in detail. However, when I accepted Jesus Christ as Lord and Savior in my life thirty-eight years ago, I ran into this fascinating story again. So, I searched and found the Scripture and it took me months to read the story, because I thought it was boring and full of repetitive verses; however, I felt compelled to read the same Scripture again.

Although I tried my best to ignore the thought, it came on stronger, until I finally asked myself, "why am I deliberately ignoring that particular Scripture, could it be that the enemy does not want me to read it?" Now it seemed obvious that it was a challenge, of which I pursued, because I never ignored a challenge. It was then that I retrieved my Bible and decided to confront the demon head-on, that was trying to hinder me from reading that Scripture, and I immediately forgot all about the previous obstacles and breezed through (Daniel Chapter 3 KJV) speedily.

I saw Real Faith in Action after reading that Scripture and had not been the same since. This powerful Scripture is a must read, because it will usher you into the arms of God, after you had seen how God displayed His power on behalf of those three young men who trusted in Him. There was no doubt in my mind that He would have done the same thing for me, and others when we put our faith and trust in Him. My own experience with God confirmed that my God is truly REAL!

The Burning Fiery Furnace

Readers, I present to you, the story of the Burning Fiery Furnace, depicted in the Book of (Daniel chapter 3 verses 1 through 30 KJV) in the Old Testament, which my husband and I also read and researched, during the time of our reading throughout the entire Bible. I chose to share this amazing story because our lives had never been the same ever since we read it through. I am encouraging all my readers to read the Bible throughout its entirety. By doing so, they will get the full understanding of what God will do for them when they applied His Principles to their daily lives.

By choice, I have chosen not to record the names of the characters; nor recording that "king" in lower case. This is my take from the Burning Fiery Furnace story:

"The Kings Image of Gold"

A certain king made an image of gold whose height was sixty cubits and the breadth six cubits. He then invited the princes, the governors, and the captains, the judges, the treasurers, the counsellors, the sheriffs, and all the rulers of the providences to attend the dedication of the golden image. On the day of the dedication, all the people stood before the golden image. Then a herald cried aloud, "O people, nations, and languages! Whenever you hear the cornet, flute, harp, sackbut, psaltery, dulcimer, and all kinds of music, you fall and worship the golden image that the king had set up; and whoever does not fall, and worship will immediately throw into the midst of a burning fiery furnace."

As this exercise took place, there were three young men that disobeyed the king's decree by refusing to fall and served his gods nor worshipped the golden image. There were informers who told the king, that these three men did not serve his gods nor worshipped the golden image that the king had set up. They also told the king the names of the three young men who disobeyed him, and he was furious!

Then the king in his rage and fury commanded them to bring the three men to him, so they brought the men to the king. The king asked them: "Is it true, and he addressed all three of them by their names; that you did not serve my gods, nor worshipped the golden image, that I had set up?"

This time the king repeated the decree himself to the three young men, how they should fall and worship the golden image when they heard the music, with a warning that if they did not fall and worship the golden image which he had made, they would be immediately cast into the midst of a burning fiery furnace. He further threatened, "and who is that God that shall deliver you out of my hands?"

The three young men answered and said to the king: "We have no need to answer you in this matter. If that is the case, our God whom we serve will deliver us from the burning fiery furnace, and He will also deliver us out of your hand, O king. But if not, let it be known unto you, O king, that we will not serve your gods, nor will we worship your golden image which you had set up."

The king became very furious, and the expression he had on his face was changed towards them, therefore he gave a command that they should heat the furnace seven times more than it was usually heated, and he commanded certain mighty men of valor who were in his army, to bind the three young men and cast them into the midst of the burning fiery furnace.

The king ordered his strong soldiers to bound the three young men in their coats, their trousers, their turbans, and their other garments and throw them into the midst of the burning fiery furnace, but the bounded men were safe, because they put their trust in the Most-High God. When humanity obeys the principles of God, and put their trust in Him, He will appoint His angels to watch over them, therefore nobody can hurt them. The angel loose the three young men and all four men were walking into the fire, when the king looked up and saw them.

Therefore, because the king's command was urgent, and the furnace was exceedingly hot, the flames of the fire killed those men of valor that picked up the three young men, and those three young men fell, bound into the midst of the burning fiery furnace; only that they never knew that God had already cooled the midst of the fiery furnace.

Suddenly, the king was astonished and rose in haste and asked his counsellors: "Did we not cast three men bound into the midst of the burning fiery furnace?" They answered and said to the king, true, O king, "Look! he answered, I see four men loosed, walking in the midst of the fire; and they are not hurt, and the form of the fourth is like the Son of God."

These are the benefits that humanity will receive when they walk in the principles of God and put their trust in Him. The king came near to the mouth of the burning fiery furnace, and addressed the three young men by their names, followed by, "servants of the most-high God, come out and come here." Then the three young men came from the midst of the fire and went to the king. The princes, governors, and captains, and the king's counsellors, saw those three young men, upon whose bodies the fire had no power, nor was a hair of their head singed, neither were their coats changed, nor the smell of fire had passed on them.

The king said Blessed be the God of these three young men, again he addressed them by their names who had sent His angel, and delivered His servants that trusted in Him, and had changed the king's word, and yielded their bodies, that they might not serve nor worship any god, except their own God. Then the king made a decree in the favor of God, Saying:

"I make a decree, that every people, nation, and language, who speaks anything amiss against the God of these three young men, shall be cut into pieces and their houses shall be made a dunghill: "Because there is no other GOD that can deliver after this sort!"

Finally, it took all that drama, for the king to voluntarily agreed, that the true and living God was mightier than his fire. He also learned that after heating his fire seven times the norm; it was no match to the power of our true and living God. The king found out the hard and humiliating way that his hands were too short to box with God; so, he surrendered, accepted his agonizing defeat, and promoted the three young men in the province of the country.

When we put our faith and trust in God, He will deliver us from our enemies and put them to open shame and public humiliation, just as He did to the king when the fourth man appeared into the midst of the burning fiery furnace, which he immediately affirmed that the form of the fourth was like the son of God. Not only that, but God had also cancelled the king's word permanently by cooling down the fire so that his assassination attempts for the three young men went invalid.

Our God will cancel every plan of the enemy when we put our

trust in Him. All our praises belong to God, I had been repetitively, encouraging you throughout this book, that "God is Real," now you had read it for yourself through the trial of the burning fiery furnace. God will do the same for you if you declare Him as your Lord and Savior and put your trust in him totally. Delight in the Lord and He will grant you the desires of your heart.

God Revealed His Impressive Power Through the Fourth Man

"This story had changed our lives forever; from the day we read this passage of Scripture, our Faith in Father God had grown much stronger, and our lives had never been the same!" It is my desire to encourage all my readers to read the Bible throughout its entirety. It would be more interesting to achieve your goal with a reading partner.

During our reading and studying of the Holy Bible, we looked forward to our beverage breaks for discussions and analysis. Please do not attempt to read too many chapters at a time, unless you got trap with a delightful story, because sometimes you will. Believe me, it happened to us. There are so many stories, but the Book of Daniel had stolen my heart for years. Whenever Daniel and his three friends sought God's assistance in any situation, they always obtained positive results. Likewise, when my husband and I prayed for others, God always honors our requests. The faith of these three men confirmed what we believed all this time, which escalated our faith to a much higher dimension in God.

The fourth man that the king saw in the burning fiery furnace had impacted our lives tremendously. The three bound men loosed and walking in the fire depicted the solidarity of their faith in their true and living God. Their trust in the Almighty God guaranteed their safety. When we put our faith and trust in God, we would be in the same category, no less, because God protects everyone who puts their trust in Him. Our God will not leave us comfortless in any situation when we put our trust in Him.

So, now that it had proven openly that our Father, God is Real, which was obvious when the king saw four men walking loosed into the burning fiery furnace. He was undoubtedly convinced that the true and living God was greater than his idols and his golden image was defeat by the power of God. There is no other God; He is the King of kings, and Lord of lords!!!

As a matter of fact, God had changed the king's decree which he had previously made, by sending His angel to cool down the fire and loosed the three bound men; and prevented the brutal fiery furnace assassination which the king had ordered for the three young men, who trusted in the true and living God, whom they worshipped. They refused to worship the king's idols, nor fell and worshipped the golden image that he had set up. That is really Faith in action!

You might recall that there were dignitaries from all over the world attending the dedication of the golden image. After reading this story, imagine yourself, if you will, standing in the front row of the audience where you could have seen the entire picture of what truly happened. You saw live and direct, exactly what the king witnessed.

He saw three bound men thrown into the midst of a burning fiery furnace, and that the men who threw them into the fire were all killed by the flames, because of the magnitude of the heat. Now, please pay special attention to what you are about to read, because it is of vital importance to this story. "Ready? Read!"

The king looked up, and suddenly he saw a FOURTH man walking in the fire with the other three men loosed, and they were not in any visible pain. One could only imagine the disappointed faces and the drama that followed it all. What a delightful experience it might have been for the guests that believed in the true and living God. God's Sovereignty stood out and declared by the king in a decree, he said: "There is no other God that can deliver after this sort!"

Now, based on what you had read and understood so far, could it be that God had gotten the attention of the dignitaries, when He displayed the deity of His awesome power in the fire at the dedication of the king's golden idol that he set up; while all his dignitaries could see that worshiping idols, and the golden image was not the right way to go, because they had no power.

Could it be that they all saw the compelling revelation of who the true and living God is? The king himself declared that: "There is no other God that can deliver after this sort!" They all heard the king when he declared that in his decree. How about you, have you considered accepting, and surrendering your life to the true and living God as your personal Savior and Lord, based on what you had read? Think about it, would you choose the gods of the king or the true and living God that the three young men had trusted in? Hold that thought!!

There are stories in the Bible that will make one laugh, will make one cry, will make one pray and ask God's forgiveness. It is of vital importance for everyone to know what is in the Bible because it is for our edification. My husband and I read the Bible throughout its entirety, and we had not been the same since. There is a wealth of information written in the Bible for the knowledge seekers who are determined to capture the wisdom of our Creator, which will be beneficial to us, as we pass on this legacy to the younger generations. If we do not pursue it, we will never know what the Creator had prepared for us. The Bible is our Blueprint/Manual that contains all our functionality. This Biblical legacy is free, the choice is yours, so let us begin before time runs out, because it will.

We should always pray and seek the wisdom, knowledge, and understanding of God before we read the Scriptures that will enable us to dissect the Scriptures accordingly, which will reveal who we are and whose we are. We purchased a juicer that came with a manual and extra instructions, informing the owner not to use the equipment before reading the manual. Likewise, the Bible is the manual for humanity.

If we read the Bible, we would not have made the mistakes that we did, because we would have known the biblical principles. God is a rewarder to those who diligently seeks him. When we put our faith and trust in God, He will reward us openly. We should read our

Bible and pray for others daily, because that is the source of our spiritual strength.

It is imperative that we focus our prayers on others rather than ourselves, which is biblical. We discovered this information while we were reading the Bible throughout its entirety. Our communication with God is through prayer. We should establish a personal relationship with God so that we can communicate with Him, instead of through our prayers only. Yes, He is closer than a brother, and we can tell Him anything, because He would never share our secrets with a best friend.

Henrietta Bowen

Always Put God First 🌿

My mission is to tell others how good God is to me, and to encourage them that He will do the same for them as well. A good platform to use is social media and other medias to tell others that the God we serve is REAL, I kid you not. On April 29, 2022; during my lunchbreak from authoring this book; I glanced on my phone to see if there were any messages that needed a response, and I saw this article popped up that I wrote on this date April 29, 2020; and it reads:

Whatever you do, please: DO NOT FORGET TO PUT GOD FIRST IN YOUR LIFE. You must pray always, and never forget to pray before you go to sleep, and when you wake up. Blessing your food is Biblical. It is particularly important that you start a relationship with God. That way, you will be in tune with Him all the time and not only when you need a 911 miracle, of course, these are bad principles that must discontinue. I am appealing to all my readers to get a reading partner and read the Bible throughout its Entirety.

I found encouraging articles that I had posted on social media from time to time. This is an amazing platform to encourage others of the importance of forgiveness which is a serious disease that is causing all sorts of sickness, even cancer and stress, among others. The antidote is just a sincere prayer from your heart, asking God to forgive you and others, of old grievances, because only God can forgive sin. You might never get sick again because your heart had been set free. God will never leave you nor forsake you. God listens in on our conversations as well. He listens to mine! I know that for a fact. Where two or three are gathered, touching anything concerning Him, He will always be in the midst to bless and to do good. I already mentioned that I was having a conversation at home with my husband and God listened in and gave me a miracle of a lifetime in a matter of seconds after we spoke.

Troubled times will come, but God will send help to you, just in time. He may not come when you want Him, but He is always on time. Sometimes your help comes in different form and shapes. Like an angel could be the mailman who delivered your mails with exceptionally good news. Could be an old friend that you had never seen in years, showed up unannounced, and offered to pay off all your overdue bills with which you were struggling. We serve a mighty God, who Is always on time!

Prior to that, you had prayed and asked the Lord to send you help, but your request was temporary delayed because God had it all figured out and planned to make it available to you on time. You see, God works on His time, which is always on time. We just need to learn how to have faith and to put our trust in Him. God is not a man that He should lie. He does not have to answer to anybody, and He always keeps His promises.

You could have gone to work while your small children were at home with their Nanny who was supervising them while they were playing in the backyard with the water hose. Unfortunately, they all went inside the house for lunch but forgot to turn off the water. Our

God that we serve, will alert your neighbor to take a little peek over your property for unknown reason, who observed the excess water flooding your yard, and alerted them immediately, hence suspended the flooding process. Our God is impressive and is Truly Real.

Ask God to Forgive Others, and Yourself. Only He Can Forgive Sin

During my dedicated reading and studying of the Scriptures, I learnt that I should put God First in everything I do, and that I should always be thankful, which is my motto to date. As I embraced the spirit of love in my heart, I found it not difficult to love others even in challenging times. Then the thought of inviting the Lord to stay permanently into my heart, was not a bad idea; so, I did!

I have asked his forgiveness of all my faults and failures, especially for every-one that I had ever done wrong. I have asked the Lord for a thorough cleansing of all unrighteousness. Since prayer is what I do, it would not be effective if there were un-forgiveness in my heart, so I surrendered, and a new spirit took control; and I had never been the same since. Likewise, I have asked the Lord to forgive everyone that did me wrong, because only God can forgive Sin. I mentioned few names that I remembered at the time, but I am quite sure that God knew and remembered everything. I spoke to Him directly from my heart and I felt the difference in my spirit, then I knew that forgiveness had taken place. Give Him Praise and Glory!

Here is one for you: Had anyone ever done you something that you thought was wrong, but you decided to forgive the person so that you could move on with your life; however, upon approaching the person, your heart skips a beat? That happened because none of us can forgive sin, and forgiveness will only take place when you personally asked God to do the forgiving on your behalf. Let us all bear in mind that only God can forgive sin, it is particularly important to remember. Get God involved and tell him all about it, and that you are asking Him please, to forgive the person. Then, and only then, a true forgiveness would have taken place.

Total forgiveness comes from the heart and only God can put His seal on it. Even when spouses decided to forgive each other and promised to move on or give it another shot; but as soon as another intense argument began, somebody always puts on their goggles and do deep-sea fishing and brought back the stench of rotten fish back to the kitchen table.

Then the nagging started all over again, and before you know it sad things started to happen. We all know what that could lead to, so the best thing is to ask God to do the forgiving for us, because He has a unique way of taking it to the sea of forgetfulness that we would remember them no more. I will not compromise the realness of God, because I have had daily proof of His existence. I am encouraging all my readers to read their Bibles and pray daily, especially for others. Please be encouraged that God loves you, no matter what situation you find yourself into. That is the reason Jesus came and died on that cruel cross at Mt. Calvary, because He wants to save us.

In case you are wondering why the continuous repetition of: "Reading the Bible throughout its entirety." The Bible you hold in your hand holds the answer to humanity's past, present and future. It is a wellspring of wisdom and divine instruction that never runs dry. Draw from this spring daily and find direction and purpose for your life. We followed this instruction and had never been the same. Just had to push as hard as I could to get the word out. Likewise, to remind everyone that, "God is Real!"

In life, there will be disappointments but that should not deter your Bible reading as soon as you are well enough to read. Do not forget that you gain spiritual strength when you read your Bible, which is the most important Book in your home. Having a Bible in your home is important, but reading it is most important, because even in hotel rooms there are Bibles for your convenience, where you can draw from your spiritual wellspring, even on vacation. That is when you really need to read and pray for others. There is no reason to pray for yourself all the time because God already knows what you need and will give you the desires of your heart. All these nuggets are in the Scriptures. It is for that reason we are inviting everyone to read the Bible throughout its entirety.

My husband and I vacationed before Covid-19, and I always wondered why every Hotel we stayed always have a Bible in our room. It was mandatory for travelers to read the Bible while they were on vacation because they had enough time to relax from all the work at home, and on the job, so that they can quit complaining about not having any time to read the Bible. I am quite sure that it could be other reasons, but that is my take! Sometimes there are excuses of not having the time to read the Bible, but that is not true. Once I was encouraging a friend to read the Bible and to always pray for others daily, but as she hesitated to respond, I stopped her before she gave me the (having no time story), so I added, before you decline, think it over for a moment; everybody uses the bathroom daily, correct? Yes, she replied, I said so, you could read your Bible instead of reading a magazine, correct? She then smiled and said, you are so right about that!

I immediately knew then that she had gotten the message. Years went by, and while we were in a conversation one day, she reminded me of the little talk that we had years ago and stated that she never forgot what I said to her about the bathroom Bible reading. With a giggle she told me that she had learnt from what I said and confirmed that it was an innovative idea. She further stated that she never thought of it that way and thanked me for the idea. She puts it into practice and had been doing that ever since I had introduced her to a better time management in reading the Bible and she has been enjoying every minute of it.

We can always find the time to pray while taking a shower, cooking, gardening, washing, loading the dishwasher, pulling weeds from the garden. Sometimes into a quiet room/closet, in our vehicles, and sometimes turn off the TV and use that time to meditate and pray for others. It is a good thing that we do not have to kneel, to pray, because it is hard to get up when I kneel. Let us not forget that God blesses us when we take time out to pray for others. We are here right now only because somebody prayed for us.

Now that it has established and that we are all convinced that everyone has the time and the ability to read the Bible and pray, what is our excuse? Sincere prayer is the antidote for every ailment in humanity, because even the doctors are encouraging their patients to pray, that is how important prayer is. It is because of the sacrifice that our Lord and Savior Jesus Christ had made for us on the cruel Cross at Mount Calvary, why we can go boldly to the throne of Grace and access the favor of God with any situation in the Name of Jesus.

After watching the movie, "The Passion of Christ," and witnessed the brutal beating and the carrying of that cross, which Jesus could have called ten thousand angels and dispersed the crowd and stopped the Crucifixion process, but instead, Christ sacrificed His life for our sins, and suffered it all alone. He gave Himself to save His own, He suffered, bled, and died alone! What a man!

Will you accept Him today? All you must do is surrender to His will, by saying, "Lord, thank you for loving me regardless of my faults and failures; please come into my heart and save me today." If you truly confess this from your heart, God will transform your life immediately and you will get your own experience with Him. God bless you as you thrive with His Amazing blessings. Whatever you do, please remember that God is Real. Stay safe and enjoy the love of God in the Name of Jesus. Amen!

Henrietta Bowen

I Am Convinced That God Is Real

The reason for this Book is to share my testimony as a COVID-19 survivor, and to inform everyone that "God is truly Real." I am the living witness, and a recipient of an amazing miracle that the Lord had done for me in our home, as my husband looked on in awe, live and direct, as it all unfolded. For your information, this encounter was record earlier.

Furthermore, I would be rather selfish and ungrateful if I failed to record the impressive love that the Lord had displayed in my life. Miracles after miracles along with the one eyewitness miracle that I had just mentioned. You had read about these miraculous events earlier, but I would really like others to know about the goodness of the Lord as well. I cannot keep this to myself because it was not meant to be mine alone. I love to share, especially the best, which is the love of God. God is so Real, and I want everyone to know it for themselves.

I am persuaded that God allowed me to recover from that massive sickness called COVID-19 Delta Variant, so that I could record these extraordinary experiences into a book so that others could read all about it, while encouraging them about His abundant blessings through Grace and Mercy. Based on the knowledge gained by discovering that God is Real, I am more determined than ever to get the word out in writing, so that others could reap the same benefits as I did. I promise you that you too, will also discover that God is Real.

Sincere Faith in God Works All of The Time

My husband and I are retired, so we teamed up and read the Bible throughout its entirety. Each day as we started to read, we prayed that God's Holy Spirit would help us to understand what we read, because we will never gain insights into the truth and application of God's Word until we ask the Holy Spirit to open our minds and reveal his truth to us and applied the truth to our lives

It was then, while we were reading the Scriptures, that we got the revelation that God is Real. I have had miracles in my lifetime, but it had not revealed to me how real God was. I had listened to others testifying how they had miracles, and got heal of infirmities over the years, but never actually witnessed my own miracle until my COVID-19 supernatural experience with my husband as eyewitness.

The Bible is also a Book with miracles, but the one that captured my faith permanently, and indelibly in my heart was the burning fiery furnace. In the Book of (Daniel chapter 3: 1-30, KJV.) I saw faith in action by those three young men who told king Neb, when he threatened to throw them in the burning fiery furnace, and bragged, "and who is that God who shall deliver you out of my hands?"

They answered, we are not careful to answer you in this matter. If it be so, our God whom we serve, will deliver us from the burning fiery furnace, and He will deliver us out of your hands. But if not, let it be known unto you, that we will not serve your gods, nor worship the golden image that you had set up. The king got angry and ordered that the furnace should heat seven times than the norm and he commanded the most-mighty men that were in the army to bind them and cast them into the midst of the burning fiery furnace and they all fell, bound into the midst of the fire. The fire was so hot that the flames killed the men that threw them in. But wait a minute, something strange had happened. As the king looked on, he saw something strange that was about to change his perspective towards the True and Living God! He was astonished and arose hastily and asked his counsellors; did not we cast three bound men into the fire? They confirmed, yes! He said look, I see four men untied walking in the fire with no hurt, and the form of the fourth, looks like the Son of God.

What a mighty God we serve!!! Hallelujah to the Lamb of God!!! God is Real!!! The king called out and addressed the men personally by their names and said, come out and come here! They did as he requested; and the princes, governors, and captains, and the king's counsellors, being together saw these men upon whose bodies the fire had no power, nor was a hair of their head singed, neither were their coats changed, nor the smell of fire had passed on them.

The king then said, blessed be the God of these three men, who have sent His angel, and delivered His servants that trusted in Him, and have changed the king's word, and yielded their bodies, that they might not serve nor worship any god, except their own God. Therefore, I make a decree, that every people, nation, and language which speak anything amiss against the God of these three men, shall cut into pieces, and their houses shall become a dunghill: Because there is no other God that can deliver after this sort. Then he promoted the three men in the province of his city. What a mighty God we serve!!!

As you think about what happened in the midst of the burning fiery furnace, and if you were truly following that supernatural event that took place as those three men fell down into the midst of the burning fiery furnace, you would have remembered that there were only three men that were cast into the fire, but the king saw a fourth man, also into the fire and they were all loosed and walking into the supposedly hot fire. Let this sink in for a while.

Ladies and Gentlemen this is something that we all should rejoice over, knowing that our God that we serve always watches over us. He will never leave us alone when we put our faith and trust in Him. Remember the faith of the three men, how they were sure that their God whom they serve, would have saved them from the king's burning fiery furnace. God sent His angle to cool the fire and loosed them, hence making a mockery out of the king.

One can only imagine how flustered the king was when he saw the fourth man into the fire, while all his dignitaries were looking on the mysteries of Godliness. That is why he hurriedly declared the decree of confirmation of his belief whilst proclaiming a ban with a threat on all unbelievers during that time.

Sincere Thanks to Our Readers 🌾

You have read in my introduction where I promised that it was my desire that you enjoyed this comfortable read, which was long overdue, how the Almighty God miraculously rescued me from the clutches of COVID-19, and that I had a burning desire to inform every one of the grace of God, and to further stressed that God is really real, based on all my experiences as you read:

"THE JOURNEY and TESTIMONY OF A COVID-19 SURVIVOR"

My sincere thanks to you for all the time that you had vested in reading this Book, and trust that you will share the knowledge gained with friends and loved ones. In addition, my desire is that you would accept my invitation to read the Bible throughout its entirety with a reading partner. My husband and I did, it was truly a blessing to us, and we had never been the same.

God Is Real

After reading my Testimony as a COVID-19 Survivor, one would have thought that it could have been the reason for this Book, but I begged to differ! The release of this book is not about me, and it was not the author's intention to compete with this Book. However, it was necessary to tell the story to reveal the proof that God is Real, even in my life.

This Testimony had revealed the evidence that "GOD IS

REAL." He spared my life so that I could inform others of "His Grace and Mercy." I have authored this Book to encourage my readers to accept the True and living God as their Lord and Savior. You might have also noticed the repetitiveness of "Reading the Bible throughout its entirety," that is particularly valuable information. We also know that God is a rewarder to those who diligently seek Him. Would you accept Him as your Lord and Savior today? Please do not put it off, because tomorrow might be too late.

Getting The Word Out That God Is Real

I know that the Lord did not save me from COVID-19 to be cute. The thought of authoring this book came to me on the morning when I was leaving from the nursing home facility, knowing how sick I was, and the Lord miraculously restored me back to life. It was then that I developed that burning desire to let others know that God is Real, and wondered how I could get the WORD out, that "God is Real?"

If humanity only knew how real God is, they would have changed their ways of thinking, and do the right thing. Life would be so much better than it is right now. How can they know without proof? Everybody should read the Bible throughout its entirety, and they would have received the answers to various unanswered questions for themselves. Read slow, repeat a verse repeatedly if needed, but get the word in for yourself. It is better with a reading partner.

Here is an example: When Jesus was Crucified, buried, rose

from the dead; one of His own disciples said that he would not believe unless he sees the nail prints in His hands and the wound in His side, he would not believe. What did you think happened? Jesus had to show him proof of His resurrection from the dead. Biblically, he was not the only one who did not believe, but he was the only one who had spoken up.

My Testimony is trustworthy, and my husband was an eyewitness, live and direct at one of my miraculous interventions. The only wise God knew He had to do that, because if he were not there as an eyewitness when it happened, who knows; maybe; he would have doubted it too. I have heard of miracles, read of miracles, and now I have had my own miracles. How could I stay quiet with all those amazingly wonderful experiences that the Lord had done in my life? Please understand that the Author truthfully author this book.

Encouraging Others to Read the Bible

Please encourage others to read this amazing Book called the Holy Bible. I obtained my information from the King James Version (KJV), they will thank you for it. I went to Sunday School and attended Church services, with my Parents and was highly active in every area, but to read the Bible throughout its entirety, was not introduce, so I never knew that it was a requirement for all humanity. All the Sunday School students studied and recited their Scripture verses, and the teachers explained the stories of the characters involved, and we later joined the adult service where the Pastor read the Scriptures and preached from selected verses. So, consider yourself truly fortunate to have someone encouraging you to read the Bible throughout its entirety. I had never read a book that revealed my existence, who I am, and whose I am. I was ecstatic when I discovered the wealth of information that I had attained.

My Amazing Manual

I had my manual in my hand all these years and never knew it! Amazing, is it not? Just as the Samaritan woman whom, when she saw Jesus as she went to draw water at the well, and was having a conversation with Him, but when Jesus told her "You have had five husbands, and the one whom you are with now, is not your husband." Upon hearing the truth about her life, she immediately dropped her water pot and ran into town and telling everyone: Come! See a man who had told me everything that I did, is not this the Christ?

Consider this a treat! Wait until you find out what I discovered after reading the Bible throughout its entirety. Please do not read in a hurry, savor the moments, because you are in for a treat of a lifetime. Do not be in a hurry to finish, because you might miss the good parts. Every bit of information that you ever craved over the years are all recorded in the Holy Bible.

You do not have to take my word for it, just read for yourself. It is all there in black and white. It might take you a year, more or less; but please continue to the end. God bless you as you thrive for excellence in the living word of God. May the peace of God which passes all understanding dwells in your heart richly, in the Name of our Lord and Savior, Jesus Christ. Amen!!!

Henrietta Bowen

70

Dedication and Acknowledgment 🖋

To our Great God Almighty, Jesus Christ our Lord, and Savior,

and The Holy Spirit, whom is the reason for my existence.

To my darling husband Herbert

for his constant love and support

in every area of my life.

To our amazing daughter Alesia

who shares her unconditional

love without reservation.

To our Niece Pastor Marcia Hines and Family

To Jennifer and Alva, our siblings

From other Parents.

To all our Children and their Families
Yvonne, Greig, Carter, Nakia, Keno, and Alesia
Our Extended Family - Children from other Parents
Claudia, Amelia, and Sherie
Close Family Friends
Ms. Brady and Family, The Dickson Family
Beverly and Family, Richard, and Family
Gayle and Family, Patrick, and Family
Yvonne and Family
To Ms. Brady and everyone who prayed for my speedy
Recovery, I am pleased to inform you that God had
Upgrade your requests to a lightning recovery. Thanks!
I also want to thank my son Carter for his love and support of my
writing

Finally, my husband Herbert has been my heartbeat
throughout this project, and I cannot thank him
enough for his contribution.

Henrietta Bowen

A Picture of my rose bush!

From my garden

Pictures of Henrietta on the left in the size 10 dress, and her daughter Alesia on the right.

A picture of Henrietta and her husband Herbert

Henrietta, Herbert and Alesia

Henrietta, Herbert, and Alesia

.

Henrietta Bowen

Lightning Source UK Ltd.
Milton Keynes UK
UKHW020617230223
417507UK00010B/51

9 798218 149864